to _____

from _____

Prayers

for Life

GARY WILDE & MARGARET ANNE HUFFMAN

PUBLICATIONS INTERNATIONAL, LTD.

Margaret Anne Huffman is an award-winning journalist and former lifestyle editor of the Shelby News. She has written and contributed to eighteen books, including: *Simple Wisdom, A Moment with God for Mothers,* and *Everyday Prayers for Grandmothers.*

Gary Wilde is a full-time freelance author and editor who has written numerous books, educational materials, and magazine articles on religious and self-help issues. One of his ongoing projects is editing the devotional quarterly, *Quiet Hour.*

Louis Weber, C.E.O.
Publications International, Ltd.
7373 North Cicero Avenue
Lincolnwood, Illinois 60646

Permission is never granted for commercial purposes.

Manufactured in China.

8 7 6 5 4 3 2 1

ISBN: 0-7853-3818-7

Contents

❀ ❀ ❀ ❀

Everyday Prayers

This is the day that the Lord has made; let us rejoice and be glad in it.

—PSALM 118:24

Today: Cause for Celebration

* * * *

With boldness, wonder, and expectation, I greet you this morning, God of sunrise. Gratefully, I look back to all that was good yesterday and in hope, face forward, ready for today.

Good Morning

* * * *

Good morning, God! We greet you with our many morning faces. We arise sometimes grumpy, sometimes smiling, sometimes prepared, sometimes behind. Always may we turn to you first in our family prayer. Bless us today and join us in it.

On the Job Together

❖ ❖ ❖ ❖

Join us at work, Lord, and in our insecurities about it; getting to and from it; in our triumphs and masteries over it; and short cuts and temptations through it. Work, amazingly, is where we spend most of our time.

෴

The Most Important Things

❖ ❖ ❖ ❖

Bless this office, where I spend so much of my time each day. In all the work I do, let me never forget my life's true priorities: family, friends, and the will of God.

Bless My Work

* * * *

All work can be good, Lord, for you can upgrade
the most mundane, difficult, or nerve-wracking
job into one that matters. God of all skills and
vocations, bless and inspire my work; deliver me
from boredom and laziness.

What About the Kids?

* * * *

Childhood is a treasure, and we working
parents fear we're squandering it as we hire
strangers to share and mold it. Guide our
choices, Lord. Hold our children in
your hands while we're gone.

The Blessing of Work

* * * *

What a blessing, Almighty One, to be able to
earn a living for the family! To be free of worry
about what they will eat, or what they will
wear, or where they will sleep. You have given us
so much: house, flowers, table and chairs, even a
video camera to help us remember these days
that are flying by so quickly. Yes, you have given.
And your gifts are a serious calling: Show us
how to give in return!

Pulled Apart

• • • •

Like the turkey wishbone, God of wholeness,
I am being pulled apart by job, family, home,
errands, friends, and my needs. I'm preoccupied
with what I am not doing and feel the pull to do
it all. Help me choose wisely. Remind me to
negotiate on the job and at home for the time
I need in both places. Remind me, O God, to
negotiate with myself for a leaner lifestyle, for I
am part of the pull. In the tugging days ahead,
be the hinge that keeps my life's parts
synchronized in harmonious movement,
not split apart at all.

Simply Sitting

✦ ✦ ✦ ✦

O God, my days are frantic dashes between
have to, ought, and should. There is no
listening bone in me. Lead me to a porch step
or a swing, a chair or a hillside, where I can be
restored by sitting, Lord, simply sitting. With
you there to meet me, sitting places become
prime places for collecting thoughts, not to
mention fragmented lives.

For This Moment

❖ ❖ ❖ ❖

Bless these next few, short moments in my day before the next problem arises. And may I remember, in all my busy-ness, that the best time to seek you is always the same: now, right now.

∽

Well-Earned Rest

❖ ❖ ❖ ❖

Lord, bless this time of recreation. May we see that it is much more than another form of employment. It is a time to pull back and relax, to honor what you highly value—after work: rest.

PRAYERS FOR LIFE ※ *17*

Balanced Diet

✦ ✦ ✦ ✦

In these nutrition-infomercial times, prepare
me a table of pleasurable moderation. And,
Lord of salads and sundaes, assure me that
nothing in your creation is itself bad; as always,
it's what I do with it that determines its value.
Be with me at the smorgasbord.

Grace

✦ ✦ ✦ ✦

Bless this food. And let it remind us once again
that the soul, like the body, lives and grows
by everything it feeds upon.
Keep us drinking in only the good and
the pure, for your glory. Amen.

Sound Sleepers

❖ ❖ ❖ ❖

Security, loving God, is going to sleep in the assurance that you know our hearts before we speak and are waiting, as soon as you hear from us, to transform our concerns into hope and action, our loneliness into companionship, and our despair into dance.

∿

Blessing for This Night

❖ ❖ ❖ ❖

The day has been long, Lord, but that's water under the bridge. Bless me now with stillness and sleep. I sigh and turn over, knowing that night will usher in the day with new joys and possibilities, gifts from your ever-wakeful spirit.

Bless This Home

❁ ❁ ❁ ❁

Surely goodness and mercy shall follow me all the days of my life, and I shall dwell in the house of the Lord my whole life long.

—Psalm 23:6

Love-Built Home

❖ ❖ ❖ ❖

Bless all that happens here, O God, planner and
builder. May we find laughter and love and
strength and sanctuary. Bless all who visit our
love-built home, family and companions with
whom we can grow. May we, like you,
offer shelter and welcome.

❧

The Faces of Love

❖ ❖ ❖ ❖

Bless my family, Lord. They are a gift from you,
evidence of your unwillingness for me to be
alone. Until I see you face to face, may the faces
of those I love be to me as your own.

Bless This Mess

❖ ❖ ❖ ❖

The house is a mess, Lord, and because of it, my attitude is a matching mood. Like handwriting on the wall of my grumpy heart, I got your message: 'Tis far wiser to hunt first crocuses on spring days than lost socks in the laundry; to sweep leaves into piles for jumping than grunge in a corner; to chase giggles rising from a child's soul like dandelion fluff than dust balls beneath beds. Bless, O Lord, this wonderful mess, and send me out to play.

Sanctuary

* * * *

Source of all life and love, let this family be a place of warmth on a cold night, a friendly haven for the lonely stranger, a small sanctuary of peace in the midst of swirling activity. Above all, let its members seek to reflect the kindness of your own heart, day by day.

Refuge

* * * *

Enter and bless this family, Lord, so that its circle will be where quarrels are made up and relationships mature, where failures are forgiven and new directions found.

Trapeze Artists

❖ ❖ ❖ ❖

Drawn like moths to flame, kids lead us new places. Guide me, pathfinding God, for I'm an aerialist leaping from bar to bar. For seconds, I'm holding neither old nor new: It's impossible to grasp a second bar while holding the first. Parents understand. We can't embrace kids' growth while requiring them to stay the same. Help me teach my kids how to swing on their bars—have standards, goals, a living faith. Steady me as I help them soar, for holding them back says I think they can't. No matter what today is like, tomorrow will be different. Help me, and the kids, live gracefully in between.

For Our Family

* * * *

*May your eyes look kindly upon this family,
Lord, for we need your love and guidance in our
lives. This is a family that seeks to do the right
things—to work hard for a living, to raise up
children who will contribute to society, and to
be a blessing in our neighborhood. But we know
we need your constant help to do these things.
May we be filled with love and happiness—all
of us who live in this home: by fulfilling our
responsibilities, day in and day out; by being
accountable in all our actions; by giving
whenever we can, even when it hurts;*

by nurturing warmth and understanding among us. And by always looking out for the best interests of others. Please grant our requests according to your great goodness.

Message of Giggles

Bless the children, God of little ones, with their giggles and wide-eyed awe, their awaking assumption that today will be chock-full of surprises, learning, and love. Neither missing nor wasting a minute, they take nothing for granted, a message that blesses us. We will go and do likewise.

Tending a Marriage

Marriage, Lord, is like a garden: You don't keep digging up a plant to see if its roots are growing! Sustain us, for there are seasons of wilted growth just as there are seasons of blossom and fruit. While ripening to become useful, may we love one another with the same strengthening trust and patience you, gardener of the world, show toward us.

Passing the Love Around

* * *

Bless us in this time of play together.
Let each child know he or she is loved. And
let us parents recognize that the love we offer
here is the same affection you have already
worked in our own hearts.

Bless My Pets

* * *

God of beasts and critters, bless them, for they
bless me even when they shed on the couch and
don't come when called. They love without
strings and share the simplest joys of walks and
catnaps, slowing me to a pace you recommend.

Perfect Parent

❖ ❖ ❖

When our children fall short of the mark and we parents fall farther still, O God, we scold ourselves to do it all, and perfectly. Give us wisdom to know that you don't ask us, nor do the children, to be perfect—just to be there.

For the Children

❖ ❖ ❖

Bless these children, God. Keep them growing in mind and body. Keep them ever moving and reaching out toward the objects of their curiosity. And may they find, in all their explorations, the one thing that holds it all together: your love.

Loving Our Neighbors

Do not neglect to show hospitality to strangers, for by doing that some have entertained angels without knowing it.

—Hebrews 13:2

Let Me Help

◆ ◆ ◆ ◆

Help me to see with new eyes today—especially
the burden of care that others harbor within
them. Grant me insight to see beyond smiling
faces into hearts that hurt. And when I
recognize the pain, Lord, let me reach out.

The Courage to Be

◆ ◆ ◆ ◆

I wish to be of service, Lord. So give me courage
to put my own hope and despair, my own doubt
and fear at the disposal of others. For how could
I ever help without first being simply . . . real?

Minding Our Manners

◆ ◆ ◆ ◆

It's hard to be pleasant these rude,
road-raging days. Everyone's too immersed
in their own concerns to be mannerly or kind.
Encourage me to get in the first words of
"please," "thanks," and "excuse me"; nudge me
to be first to take turns on the road, in the store,
at work. Maybe good manners will be as
catching as rude ones; may I, with your
guidance, be first to pass them on.

Neighborly Blessing

* * * *

Bless my neighbor today. But keep me from
telling him that I've got his good in mind.
Only let him discover it in my smile, in my
encouraging words, and in my helping hand.

Blessing for Peacemakers

* * * *

Bless me with a peacemaker's kind heart and a
builder's sturdy hand, Lord, for these are mean-
spirited, litigious times when we tear down with
words and weapons first and ask questions later.
Help me take every opportunity to compliment,
praise, and applaud as I rebuild peace.

Room for One More

❖ ❖ ❖ ❖

Opposites don't attract nearly as often as they
repel, if we are to believe the headlines.
Pick a race, color, creed, or lifestyle, Lord of all,
and we'll find something to fight about.
Deliver us from stereotypes. Inspire us to spot
value in everyone we meet. As we dodge the
curses and hatred, we are relieved there is room
for all of us beneath your wings. Bless our
diversity; may it flourish.

Different Is Lovely

❖ ❖ ❖ ❖

We want to belong and go to great lengths to fit
anonymously in, forgetting we are like
snowflakes, no two, thank God, alike. Each
snowflake and child of yours is the same in
essence but different in form. Bless our unique,
one-of-a-kind value. We are heartened to know
that no one is created more special. It is not
your way to make one snowflake, or one
person, better than another.

Lovable Differences

◆ ◆ ◆ ◆

Bless our differences, O Lord. And let us love across all barriers, the walls we build of color, culture, and language. Let us turn our eyes upward and remember: The God who made us all lives and breathes and moves within us, untouched by our petty distinctions. Let us love him as he is, for he loves us just as we are.

All One

◆ ◆ ◆ ◆

You have said: We are all one. So when I am tempted to separate, alienate, exasperate my sisters and brothers, remind me: We are all one.

Forgiveness

✦ ✦ ✦ ✦

Let me know the satisfaction of forgiving today,
O Lord. I have held my peace, doused my anger.
Now it is time to extend my hand.

❧

A Second Look

✦ ✦ ✦ ✦

Give me eyes, O God, to take a second look at
those who think, act, and look different from
me. Help me take seriously your image of them.
Equip me with acceptance and courage as I hold
out a welcoming hand, knowing that you are
where strangers' hands meet.

Holidays & Celebrations

Clap your hands,
all you peoples;
shout to God with
loud songs of joy.

—PSALM 47:1

Grace for Our Feast

* * * *

We gather around this feasting table, humbled
by our bounty, Lord of abundant life; we have so
much more than we need. We confess that we
are poised, fork in hand, ready to overdo.
Help us learn how to live as grateful, if
overstuffed, children—delighted, surprised, and
generous with the sharing of our good fortune.
Bless us now as we enjoy it amid food, friends,
and family. We give the heartiest thanks for
your diligent, steadfast care.

Blessing for a New Year

* * * *

The slate is clean, Lord, the calendar as bare as the Christmas tree. Bless the New Year that beckons. We sing of you as help in ages past but need to know you as hope for years to come. Help us face what we must, celebrate every triumph we can, and make any changes we need. We're celebrating to the fullest this whistle-blowing, toast-raising moment, for it is the threshold between the old and the new us.

How Beautiful You Are

Happy birthday to you! That was a good day,
and you were there. Everyone who saw you
thought: "How beautiful!" So take a moment in
front of the mirror: Still beautiful, no matter
how you look. For God sees only your loveliness.
From day one.

Caught up in Traditions

We're caught up in well-worn, comfy traditions,
Lord. Keep them worthy, for like a deer path
through the forest, they lead us forward and
back. Thank you for the divine love and
holiness found in the ordinary.

An Easter Meal Grace

❀ ❀ ❀ ❀

We are celebrating today, O God, a mixture of
bunnies hiding colored eggs and angels rolling
away stones. Join us as we gather to share
a meal and ponder both, enjoying the one
and giving thanks for the other. Bless those at
this table savoring the food and the message
of this day. Remind us, too, Lord of unexpected
appearances, that this also is the season of
spring, a time when rebirth is not so surprising
after all. Send us after lunch into the yard
where, hiding colored Easter eggs for the
children, we may understand anew
what this day really means.

Blessings on the Anniversary Couple

◆ ◆ ◆ ◆

There is no greater mystery than love, Lord of covenants and promises. We are in its presence on this anniversary day. Bless those who live, day after day after ordinary day, within the fullness of married love, surely one of life's greatest mysteries. Bless them as they honor their past, even while they create a future. Let them bask in the pleasures and applause of today, when we bow before their accomplishments, which, like the rings we read on the inner souls of trees, are an inspiration and blessing to us all.

A Blessing for Memorial Day: The Gift of History

Surrounded by a community of headstones, we remember and mourn, celebrate and play, God of history and future. We place our bouquets on overgrown graves and our picnic lunches on family reunion tables. And we feel grateful for our history written by strangers fallen in battle to insure our freedom-filled lives of safety. Our ancestors' efforts are remembered throughout our lives in strengths, names, and accomplishments that we now pause and honor. Bless our picnics and parties as we join in the parade of those remembering, those remembered.

A Small Prayer While Wrapping Presents

* * * *

Tangled in tape, lists, and holiday wrappings,
we are all thumbs of excitement! Bless the
surprises we've selected, wrapped, and hidden.
Restore us to the joy of anticipation. We want to
be surprised, too. Our wish lists include the gift
of peace possibilities, of ears to hear a summons
and eyes to spot another's need or triumph, of
being able to make a difference. As we cut and
tape, God of surprises, remind us to keep in
touch with the gift's recipient after the wrapping
papers are long gone and the ornaments packed.

Through Troubles & Transitions

❀ ❀ ❀ ❀ ❀

Do not worry about anything,
but in everything by prayer
and supplication with
thanksgiving let your requests
be made known to God.

—PHILIPPIANS 4:6

Reflections of Light

• • • •

Held up to your light, our broken hearts can become prisms that scatter micro-rainbows on the wall. Our pain is useless as it is, redeeming God, just as a prism is a useless chunk of glass until light passes through it. Remind us that the smallest ray of sun in a shower can create a rainbow. Use our tears as the showers and your love as the sun. Looking up, we see the tiniest arches of hope in the lightening sky.

The Whole Package

✦ ✦ ✦

*Dear God, complaints sometimes come first
before I can feel free to love you. Sometimes you
seem distant and unreasonable, uncaring.
Help me understand why life can be so hurtful
and hard. Hear my complaints and, in the
spirit of compassion, show me how to
move through pain to rebirth.*

～

The Next Step

✦ ✦ ✦

*Lord, give me the faith to take the next step,
even when I don't know what lies ahead. Give
me the assurance that even if I stumble and fall,*

you'll pick me up and put me back on the path.
And give me the confidence that, even if I lose
faith, you will never lose me.

❧

Unfair

✦ ✦ ✦ ✦

Life's not fair, and I stomp my foot in
frustration. The powerful get more so as the rest
of us shrink, dreams for peace are shattered as
bullies get the upper hand, and despair is a
tempting pit to fall into. Help me hold on, for
you are a God of justice and dreams, of turning
life upside down. Let me help; thanks for
listening in the meantime.

Weed Power

✦ ✦ ✦ ✦

Even in our toughest moments, Lord, we yearn
to grow into fullest flower. Give us a faith
as resilient and determined as dandelions
pushing up through pavement cracks.

Peaks and Valleys

✦ ✦ ✦ ✦

A chart of my efforts to change traces a jagged
course, Lord, like the lines on a heart-rate
monitor. Reassure me that instead of measuring
my failures, ups and downs mean simply that I
am alive and ever-changing. Help me become
consistent, but deliver me from flat lines.

Birds of a Feather

❖ ❖ ❖ ❖

*Troubles, dear Lord, have cast us loose from
assumptions and certainties, and we are
bobbing like rudderless boats on a stormy surf.
When all hope seems gone, we spot doves on the
horizon. Doves like those you sent your Noah
children to assure them the storm was nearly
over. Doves in the phone calls from friends; in
the smile of a neighbor; in the wisdom of a
caregiver or counselor; in good laughs or hearty,
cleansing tears; in the flash of a new idea, a
goal, a dream. We recognize landmarks now
and can see our way through the storm, guided
by your love-winged messengers.*

Healing Failure

✦ ✦ ✦ ✦

I blew it. Give me courage to admit my mistake, apologize, and go on. Keep me from getting stuck in denial, despair, and, worst of all, fear of trying again. In your remolding hands, God of grace, failures can become feedback and mistakes can simply be lessons in what doesn't work. Remind me that perfection means "suited to the task," not "without mistakes." There's a world of difference.

Fresh Air

✦ ✦ ✦ ✦

Today I need your help, God. I'm feeling
the need for a breath of fresh air. The old
habits and attitudes I've clung to for so long
seem stale and worn out. Renew me from
the inside out, starting now!

∿

What to Do?

✦ ✦ ✦ ✦

Someone I care about is suffering, Lord,
and I feel helpless. Assure me that a little
means a lot and that I'm sharing your healing
love in my notes and visits. If you need me to do
more, send me. I am like dandelion fluff,
small but mighty in possibility.

Hopeful Night

* * * *

In the midst of mourning life's troubles,
you come to us. In the darkness, your spirit
moves, spreading light like a shower of stars
against a stormy night sky.

*

Darkest Before
the Dawn

* * * *

Teach us to know, God, that it is exactly at the
point of our deepest despair that you are the
closest. For at those times we can finally admit
we have wandered in the dark, without a clue.
Yet you have been there with us all along.
Thank you for your abiding presence.

Grains of Hope

* * * *

When trouble strikes, O God, we are restored by
small signs of hope found in ordinary places:
friends, random kindness, shared pain
and support. Help us collect them like
mustard seeds that can grow into a
spreading harvest of well-being.

❧

Problems, Problems

* * * *

You have made things problematic again, Lord,
and I need to see that all this upheaval can be a
good thing. Help me, Lord. And thank you for
showing me that a thoroughly comfortable
existence can rob me of real life.

Making New Places for God

* * * *

Change is inevitable, Lord, we know. Help us to
accept: If we view each transition as an opportunity to experience your faithfulness, we make
new places in our lives for spiritual growth.

Always With Us

* * * *

We know there is no greater burden than to
think no one cares or understands. That is why
the promise of your presence is so precious to us,
you who said: "Remember, I am with you
always, to the end of the age."

Everyday Miracles, Pleasures & Joys

You show me the path of life.
In your presence there is
fullness of joy; in your right
hand are pleasures forevermore.

—PSALM 16:11

In Praise of the Usual

＊＊＊＊

So much to celebrate, Lord: waking to dawn
gilding trees; squeezing fresh orange juice, its
zest clinging to my hands all day; making a new
friend, talking to an old one; watching the first
leaf bud, raking the last. Each day's turning
brings gifts from you to celebrate.

Ordinary Miracles

＊＊＊＊

When we doubt your miracle-making power,
Lord, show us the ordinary miracles of seasons,
of hope regained, of love from family and
friends, and of surprises that turn out
miraculous simply by remaking our lives.

Lasting Legacy

◆ ◆ ◆

"Put off today and think of tomorrow."
How's that for a motto, Lord? Fine, for it invites
me to forget past errors, ignore present to-do
lists, and look ahead. What will I—family,
friends, you—remember? That I did laundry
instead of reading to a child or talking to a
friend? What will endure? Time I gave
committees instead of family and self?
Chores I did instead of picnicking, walking,
sitting on a log? The answer prompts another
motto, inspiration from you: Cherish the
moment, celebrate today.

The True Excitement

* * * *

When I'm bored, remind me: This is the
excitement of life—darkness alternating with
light, down dancing with up, and inactivity
being absolutely essential—as prelude—to the
most fulfilling experiences of all.

In Stillness

* * * *

I know that faith is what keeps me
moving forward. But sometimes, too,
my trust allows a leisure like this. For you,
God, are the one who upholds all things. Even
as I sit here in stillness, your breath keeps me
breathing, your mind keeps me thinking,
your love keeps me yearning for home.

Puddle Prayers

❖ ❖ ❖ ❖

Pardon my muddy feet, God of raindrops and wriggle worms. I've been outside. Splashing in puddles like a child does to rediscover your creation: cloak of fog, spiderweb weavings, birds of different feathers dining peacefully together. I get too busy to enjoy it. Thank you for this mud-liscious day when I am brought to my knees in awe, the best place to meet you—as any child knows. I plan to pray barefoot from now on, curling my toes and stretching toward you, becoming like a child, as you encourage, so each day can be a whole-body experience.

For it is because you are, that I am.

Small Miracles

* * * *

*Bless you, Lord! The heavens declare your glory;
the skies proclaim your mighty power. And here
I am, looking up into those vast regions,
knowing that the tiniest cell in my body is a
most glorious miracle, as well. Bless you, Lord!*

❧

Grains of Sand

* * * *

*We are surprised by joy, God of re-creation,
when we see despair outwitted by simple acts of
love as small as grains of sand. Keep us search-
ing, believing, and building upon them, realizing
that grains of sand make dune, shore, and desert.*

No Waiting

* * * *

Will tomorrow be less hectic and more inclined toward joy? Will I be less tired? God help me, I'm not waiting to find out. In your creation, joy can be found anytime, but mostly now. Keep reminding me that now is all of life I can hold at any moment. It cannot be banked, invested, hoarded, or saved. It can only be spent.

Signs of Hope

✦ ✦ ✦ ✦

*We know you, Lord, in the changing seasons: in
leaves blazing gently in fall beauty; in winter's
snow sculptures. We know you in arid desert
cactus bloom and in migration of whale and
spawn of fish and turtle. In the blending of the
seasons, we feel your renewing, steadfast care,
and worries lose their power to overwhelm.
The list of your hope-filled marvels is endless,
our gratitude equally so.*

Taking Care of Today

◆ ◆ ◆ ◆

*Slow my pell-mell race into the future,
everlasting God, for I am racing past the
exquisite moment, which, like a snowflake, is
unlike any other and never to be retrieved.*

༄

Extreme Love

◆ ◆ ◆ ◆

*You are everywhere, Lord, and we're comforted
to be enfolded as we move through life's
extremes. You are with us in birthings and
dyings, in routine and surprise, and in stillness
and activity. We cannot wander so far in any
direction that you are not already there.*

Thanks-living

• • • •

Some prayers are best left unfinished, God of
abundance, and this will be an ongoing
conversation between us. Each day, I discover
new gifts you offer me, and the list of reasons to
be thankful grows. As I accept your gifts and live
with them thankfully, guide me to become a
person who shares with others so that they, too,
can live abundantly. May someone, somewhere,
someday say of me, "I am thankful to have
this person in my life."

Thank you for the friends around
table "" you for the love, friendship,
fellowship and laughter that they
bring to all our lives. And we all say.

Photo credits:

FPG International: Laurance B. Aiuppy: 39; Willard Clay: 74; Color Box: 8, 42; Barbara Peacock: 28; Gail Shumway: 25; Telegraph Colour Library: 36, 56; **SuperStock:** Title page, 13, 20, 66, 78; **Tony Stone Images:** Ken Graham: 52; Richard Kaylin: 62; Charles Krebs: 70; Pat O'Hara: 46; Ian O'Leary: 32; James Randklev: 49; Andy Roberts: 60; Peter Timmermans: 17.